T0163704

THE LITTLE BOOK OF
MAN CITY

Independent and Unofficial

SIXTH EDITION

EDITED BY
DAVID CLAYTON

First published by Carlton Books in 2002
Updated editions 2008, 2010, 2014, 2018

This edition published in 2023 by OH!
An Imprint of Welbeck Non-Fiction Limited,
part of Welbeck Publishing Group.
Based in London and Sydney.
www.welbeckpublishing.com

Compilation text © Welbeck Non-Fiction Limited 2022
Design © Welbeck Non-Fiction Limited 2022

A CIP catalogue record of this book is available from the British Library.

ISBN 978 1 91161 035 9

Printed in China

10 9 8 7 6 5 4 3 2 1

CONTENTS

INTRODUCTION

Manchester City: has there ever been another club like them?
Relegation, promotion, manager after manager, overflowing with
silverware during the 1960s then nothing for 30 years. Adored
by their amazing, wonderful and loyal supporters, this old club
has had more than its fair share of colourful characters.

But now "typical City" have been transformed by Sheikh Mansour's
billions, which have brought back the glory days with FA Cup and
Premier League wins – and the promise of much more to come.

In this great collection of quotes, players, managers and famous
fans past and present reveal why, for them, Blue really is the
colour. From the heady days of the 1960s and 70s, to the
wilderness years of the 80s and 90s, to the transformation of the
club in 2008 there are soundbites here to satisfy every Citizen.
Players such as Colin Bell, Gio Kinkladze, Vincent Kompany,
Sergio Aguero and Phil Foden are all featured, along with a host
of managers and chairmen from Joe Mercer and Kevin Keegan
to Sheikh Mansour, Manuel Pellegrini and Pep Guardiola.

When it comes to City, with it endless dramas, opinions come
thick and fast and this book serves up quotes that are revealing
and always intriguing.

CHAPTER 1

GAFFER CHATTER

❝My mum always told me not to
go near the main road.**❞**

KEVIN KEEGAN

during his first press conference at Manchester City, June 2001

"It's a massive club.
It's just a bit sickly.**"**

JOE ROYLE

shortly after becoming manager, February 1998

❝We've got it all to look forward to. We've just got to make sure we're as good as this stadium.**❞**

KEVIN KEEGAN

surveys City's future home – the City of Manchester Stadium,
June 2001

"I keep turning the corner and bumping into somebody else I'd forgotten is here. There is a network of players here, not a squad … **"**

JOE ROYLE's

initial assessment of the 40-plus players he inherited at Maine Road, February 1999

❝Creating something new is the difficult part. To make it and build it and get everyone to follow? Amazing.**❞**

PEP GUARDIOLA

2016

❝In football, the worst things are excuses. Excuses mean you cannot grow or move forward. **❞**

PEP GUARDIOLA

not one for excuses!

❝He has a special gift for bringing out the best in players. He makes them believe in themselves.**❞**

COLIN BELL

on Malcolm Allison's "second coming", January 1979

"We went out believing we could beat anybody – it didn't matter who we turned out against. The team talks were very limited. 'Get out and play, you're better than they are, score more goals than the side you're playing.'**"**

COLIN BELL

recalls Joe Mercer's legendary leadership

❝I think football will get bigger
and bigger in this country. I think you'll see
the time – probably not in my career – when
footballers will earn as much as golfers and
tennis players and will earn fantastic
amounts of money.**❞**

FRANCIS LEE

aged 25, astutely foreseeing the game as it is today, 1971

"That division clung to us like quicksand. We were the biggest show in town wherever we went and people welcomed us with open arms… and then tried to kick us.**"**

JOE ROYLE

recalls life in Division Two, 1999

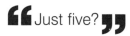**Just five?**

MANUEL PELLEGRINI

A deadpan response to City CEO, Ferran Soriano's ambition in July
2013 that City should win five trophies in the next five seasons

❝I rang my secretary and said, 'What time to do we kick off tonight?' and she said, 'Every ten minutes.'**❞**

ALAN BALL

during his troubled year as City manager, 1996

❝We've got him for free and I have to pinch myself to believe it.**❞**

KEVIN KEEGAN

on Ali Bernarbia, September 2001

❝In the end, I left before I could do any long-term damage. I regret not leaving the City fans with a positive image of me – instead, they must be bewildered. **❞**

STEVE COPPELL

following his month in charge of the Blues, 1997

" Yes, we are conceding more goals than I would like – maybe I'm not the guy for a 0–0 draw away from home. **"**

KEVIN KEEGAN

after the following run of away results: 4–2, 0–4, 4–2, 3–4, 6–2!
September 2001

❝The only time I want to see him miserable is after I've taken City to Old Trafford.**❞**

KEVIN KEEGAN

on Sir Alex Ferguson, June 2001

"Colin was the jewel in
the crown. Everything he touched
seemed to turn to gold. **"**

BOB STOKOE

Colin Bell's first manager, August 1979

"I don't care about the 'Mr Nobody' tag. I've always made my own decisions and I'm not going to change just because I'm moving to a big club. I'm going to be my own man.**"**

BRIAN HORTON

August 1993

❝It won't be long before he has our supporters hanging from the rafters.**❞**

ALAN BALL

predicting a bright future for new signing Georgi Kinkladze,
August 1995

❝Georgi Kinkladze would grace any team, at any level throughout the world. **❞**

ALAN BALL

May 1996

HEADWAITER:

"Mr Allison, your bar bill – I have to tell you, it is enormous. **"**

ALLISON:

"Is that all? You insult me. Don't come back until it's double that! **"**

MALCOLM ALLISON

enjoying the champagne lifestyle of the early 1970s

28

"It has left a stain on our playing record that will take a long time to fade, if, indeed, it is ever allowed to. **"**

MALCOLM ALLISON

after City lost 1–0 in an FA Cup 3rd round tie to Fourth Division Halifax Town, January 1980

❝I can't believe what I've seen tonight.
It was a disgrace. If we'd have scored
another goal in that atmosphere I don't think
we would have got out alive.**❞**

JOE ROYLE

after City's September 1998 visit to Millwall

❝I've had a player sent off for aggressive walking! I think I must have missed a rule change somewhere. **❞**

JOE ROYLE

bewildered by Kevin Horlock's sending-off, February 1999

❝Son, I have thought it over
and it's you and me together.
We are this bloody football club. **❞**

JOE MERCER

to Malcolm Allison

" Sometimes you have to shoot at the stars and maybe you'll hit the moon. **"**

KEVIN KEEGAN

January 2002

"If anybody's offended by seeing a backside, get real. Maybe they're just jealous that he's got a real nice tight one, with no cellulite or anything. I thought his bum cheeks looked very pert.**"**

IAN HOLLOWAY

lends his own unique view of Joey Barton's decision to bare his backside to Everton fans, 2006

❝I think he's an absolutely fantastic bloke, top geezer, and if he wants to carry a little horse on the side of the pitch, I don't care!**❞**

IAN HOLLOWAY
on Stuart Pearce's lucky mascot, "Beanie", 2008

❝Suddenly, I win the derby
and people are talking about England
again. It is absolutely pathetic.**❞**

STUART PEARCE

*responds to the adulation poured on him after beating
Man United 3–1 and not long before he took on the role
of England Under-21 boss! 2006*

“The result is an empty thing.
The result is I'm happy for the next two days
because I get less criticism and more time
to improve my team. But what satisfies
me the most in my job is to feel emotions,
the way we play.**”**

PEP GUARDIOLA

2017

"I will calmly make corrections to what they eat before matches. You need more chicken, pizza, carbohydrates. As well as a glass of wine, which isn't being served.**"**

ROBERTO MANCINI

reveals his plans to revolutionise the pre-match meal,
January 2010

❝I understand that Bobby is short for Roberto in England and the fact that the first part of my surname is also short for Mancunian is perfect. I know that the supporters have given me this name as a gesture of affection, but it is important that we win something for them this season and then many trophies in the future – then I will have given them something in return. But the nickname 'Bobby Manc' – yes, I like it a lot!**❞**

ROBERTO MANCINI

January 2010

❝Roberto [Mancini] did a great job here in Manchester, especially to win the title after so many years. We now start a new cycle.**❞**

MANUEL PELLEGRINI

says the right things after joining City, June 2013

" If someone had said two or three years ago that City would become one of the top teams in the world, no one would have believed it. **"**

ROBERTO MANCINI

May 2011

"I am finished. We have six games and he will not play in the next six games."

ROBERTO MANCINI's

patience snaps with Mario Balotelli, April 2012

❝I defend him always because Mario is a good guy, but if he doesn't change in the future he can lose all his talent. If he doesn't understand this, after two years I can't do anything… I'm very sorry for him for this.**❞**

ROBERTO MANCINI

warns Mario Balotelli that he is on the path to rack and ruin, April 2012

❝You continue to speak about this for six months, and also in the last two weeks too much, and I don't know why the club didn't stop this because I don't think it was correct. **❞**

ROBERTO MANCINI

is hurt by the rumours he will be sacked, after the FA Cup Final defeat to Wigan, May 2013

❝Success without playing the way you like to play means nothing to me.❞

PEP GUARDIOLA

arrives intending to do it his way. August 2016

"I don't want just two or three players defending or trying to score goals, I want everyone defending and everyone attacking. I want to see every player move.**"**

PEP GUARDIOLA

his philosophy laid bare, 2017

"Of course, it was so weird, a semi-final of the Champons League in an empty stadium. This achievement belongs to our fans… the club belongs to the people.**"**

PEP GUARDIOLA

acknowledging the missing fans while praising his players after
they beat Paris St Germain at an empty Etihad Stadium to reach their first
Champions League final in May 2021

CHAPTER 2

CELEBS AND PUNDITS

❝Sometimes we're good and sometimes we're bad, but when we are good, at least we are much better than we used to be and when we are bad we're just as bad as we always used to be, so that's got to be good, hasn't it?**❞**

MARK RADCLIFFE

Radio 1 DJ and City fan, November 2011

"That's it, game over!**"**

BRIAN HORTON

*commentating for ITV, announces City's demise as they go 2–0 down
in the 86th minute to Gillingham in the 1999 Play-off Final*

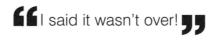

I said it wasn't over!

BRIAN HORTON

eight minutes later, as City draw level 2–2, May 1999

❝On my gravestone, the epitaph will read:
'I'd rather be here than Old Trafford.'**❞**

BERNARD MANNING

May 2002

"It's true. I think he phoned our management office. There's no way he's ever getting them. He scored against City on his debut.**"**

NOEL GALLAGHER

explains why Ryan Giggs never received complimentary tickets for a hometown Oasis concert, May 1998

❝I don't want those scally City fans round at my house putting my windows in when City are in the Third Division and blaming it all on me.**❞**

NOEL GALLAGHER

responds to suggestions he should become chairman, May 1999

❝After watching City for
50 years and working with that
Syd Little for 40, I was always going to
be a prime candidate for hospital.**❞**

EDDIE LARGE

shortly after a serious heart operation, March 2002

"Dennis Tueart was my favourite player as a kid but I treasured a framed photo of Colin Bell that I'd bought from some dodgy market stall.**"**

JOHNNY MARR

City fan, June 2002

"My five-year-old son told me he had fallen out with his best friend about City and United. We'd just been relegated to Division Two and United were winning everything, so I thought about it and decided to have a father and son talk. I said, 'You've decided to follow a team that's not going to be on television much over the next few years and

it's going to be tough.' I bit my lip, took a gulp and said, 'If you like, you can even support United.' He looked at me in horror and spat out, 'But, Dad, I could support Arsenal, I could support Newcastle, but I can't support United.' I just thought, 'Put a tag on his toe, he's a Blue for life.' **"**

JOHNNY MARR

on the trials of parenthood, June 2002

"He arrived like a giraffe on roller skates.**"**

ROB McCAFFREY's

bizarre description of Niall Quinn's equaliser in his
debut for City versus Chelsea, 1990

❝I just think Manchester City have taken us onto a new planet.❞

JOHN MOTSON

*the veteran commentator gives his considered opinion on City's
quality after a lifetime watching the game, March 2018*

“What will help City is the fact that they get big crowds, have a good ground and the best fans in the country.**”**

MARK LAWRENSON

2001

"The Kippax was basically a big shed. It was very dark and there was no lighting and a really huge roof coming down low, so it was like looking at a television screen.**"**

NOEL GALLAGHER

❝We could get into Europe this season,
or we could get relegated – that's why I
support City.**❞**

NOEL GALLAGHER

gives his view on City's return to the Premiership, July 2000

❝Maine Road was a state-of-the-art stadium with high stands and lush turf cut and carted from the best pastures in Cheshire. Before the match, the band played, 'Ours Is a Nice House, Is Ours.'**❞**

DAVE HASLAM

author of Manchester, England, *on City's 1923 move to Maine Road, 1999*

65

"In a team which has often taken your breath away, De Bruyne has been simply outstanding in every respect: 11 goals from midfield, 19 assists, wicked set-piece delivery, weight of pass, angles, mobility and tempo. What's not to like?**"**

ROBBIE SAVAGE

no controversy from Robbie as he names Kevin De Bruyne
his player of the year, March 2018

"I always kind of knew that 40 years of loyalty would be repaid somehow and I always knew that a day would come when we stagger everyone in football. It'll be nice to know that every gallon of petrol a Manchester United fan buys is going into our transfer kitty.**"**

NOEL GALLAGHER

*fuels the news that City had been taken over by
Abu Dhabi billionaire Sheikh Mansour*

" When Oasis were doing well, City were doing s**t. But now we've split, City are doing good. Maybe there are some good times ahead with City, and that'll take the pain off the band splitting up a bit. **"**

LIAM GALLAGHER

looking through blue-tinted glasses, March 2010

❝It's gone mad. Mancini's on the pitch, running around. They're all cuddling each other – they've got love bites and everything!**❞**

PAUL MERSON

Sky Sports pundit, gets as excited as the fans as City win the Premier League title, May 2012

CHAPTER 3

HEROES OF THE SHIRT

❝The sooner McMahon returns the better. I have been so stiff recently on the morning after matches that I thought rigor-mortis had set in.**❞**

PETER REID

looks forward to retirement from playing, April 1993

❝He sees you when you
can't even see yourself. **❞**

PAULO WANCHOPE

on Ali Benarbia's telepathic passing abilities, October 2001

"He's crazy! The guy's crazy, honestly. Sometimes I think he doesn't feel something. If he concedes a goal, he is calm, makes the save of his life, he is calm.**"**

PEP GUARDIOLA

on Ederson, 2022

"People said that I must have kept all the bricks that came through my window and put a snooker room on the side of my house. I did keep the bricks but I built a five-bedroom detached house in Wilmslow with them.**"**

STEVE DALEY

1979 British transfer record holder after life at Maine Road turned sour

❝I always like to assist more than scoring: it gives me another feeling; I cannot explain it. ❞

KEVIN DE BRUYNE

the typically selfless superstar trying to explain it in 2018

❝As overwhelming as it is, the time has come for me to go. And what a season to bow out. I feel nothing but gratefulness. I am grateful to all those who supported me on a special journey, at a very special club.
I remember the first day, as clear as I see the last. I remember the boundless kindness I received from the people of Manchester.**❞**

VINCENT KOMPANY

the former skipper announces his departure in 2018

"I will never forget how all Man City supporters remained loyal to me in good times and especially bad times. Against the odds you have always backed me and inspired me to never give up.**"**

VINCENT KOMPANY

on announcing his decision to leave, May 2019

❝When I do something special
the fans like me even more and I like
me even more!**❞**

ALI BENARBIA

October 2001

Interviewer:

"Have you received this sort of adulation before?**"**

"It happens at every club I play for!**"**

ALI BENARBIA

on being the fans' idol, February 2002

"Unless you've experienced thousands of people chanting your name, it's very difficult to describe how it makes you feel.**"**

SHAUN GOATER

March 2002

"Obviously, it's difficult. It's been a long time, but all good things come to an end. I want it to be this way, at a great level.**"**

DAVID SILVA

on leaving City, 2019

❝One of my main aims in life is to prove
that footballers are not the fools many
people think they are.**❞**

FRANCIS LEE

future multi-millionaire, August 1970

"I remember a game against Liverpool. I was stood on one leg hooking the ball with the other. Next thing, Tommy Smith took my standing leg away and I finished in a heap. 'Never stand on one leg when I'm around,' growled Tommy.**"**

MIKE SUMMERBEE

❝Although I feel the same thrills and disappointments as everybody else, somehow I just don't seem able to show emotion. Maybe it's a fault in my make-up but I can assure the fans I'm not devoid of feeling.**❞**

COLIN BELL

1970

85

❝It's hilarious sometimes. Even when he is angry in a match all you get from him is 'ruddy hell' or 'flipping heck'. What a player and what an example to any kid.**❞**

JOE CORRIGAN

on Colin Bell, the perfect gentleman

86

"Sergio's contribution to Manchester City over the last 10 years cannot be overstated. His legend will be indelibly etched into the memories of everyone who loves the Club and maybe even in those who simply love football.**"**

KHALDOON AL MUBARAK

on Sergio Aguero's time at City, March 2021

"My mother wanted me to be a folk dancer, so when my father went to Russia to work for three years she hid away my football boots and took me to dancing classes.**"**

GIO KINKLADZE

often seen dancing through defences, December 1995

"He's alright but he's getting some stick. It serves him right for having a flash car!**"**

PAUL DICKOV

after Kinky's high-speed car crash, 1997

89

❝I should walk away,
but I can't sometimes.**❞**

Tough defender **ANDY MORRISON**
commenting on his disciplinary problems, March 1999

" They want to talk about the game and maybe say, 'Oh, Ali Benarbia – I want to go and see him again.' I want to give them pleasure by watching me play. **"**

ALI BENARBIA

September 2001

" They deserve to be flying high. They've had all kinds of stick from over the road and they've stuck by us through thick and thin. **"**

JEFF WHITLEY

on the City fans, March 2002

"He's our club captain, he leads by example and you can't ask for any more. When it gets tough, you know he's going to be there standing strong, that lifts you and you think that if he's like that you follow the example he sets. You know if a shot's coming in he'll get his head in the way.**"**

JOEY BARTON

on Richard Dunne, 2006

"I don't think I'll ever get away from my reputation. If you tried Googling me, you know I won't get away from it. If I ever do a book – which I won't – the title will be *Don't Google Me*. I've been involved in a few things, I've held my hand up, but over the last few years I've been in a good place.**"**

CRAIG BELLAMY

painfully honest as ever, January 2009

❝The celebration is based on a kind of dance my brother usually does – I'm not sure why or where it comes from. He asked me about a month ago to do it on the pitch when I next scored, which I did, and I've done it pretty much ever since. I've seen the City fans' version in recent games – very entertaining!**❞**

CARLOS TEVEZ

on his backside jiggling celebration, January 2010

❝I didn't feel right to play, so I didn't.❞

CARLOS TEVEZ

*responds to Roberto Mancini's accusation of failing to
come on as a substitute, September 2011*

"Ten seasons with major achievements, throughout which I was able to become the top historic goalscorer and forging an indestructible bond with all those who love this club – people who will always be in my heart.**"**

SERGIO AGUERO

bids farewell to the club he loves, March 2021

"Why always me?**"**

MARIO BALOTELLI's

T-shirt, after the fireworks incident at his house, October 2011

❝All his teams play attractive football,
that is what people want to see.
You pay for tickets to go to football to see
something great, and he is the kind of
manager who can do it. **❞**

SAMIR NASRI

on Manuel Pellegrini's credentials, June 2013

"Wayne Rooney is a very good player, but not the best in Manchester.**"**

MARIO BALOTELLI

has a dig at the United striker

"When I first came to Manchester, I felt like when I was in Barcelona, at Espanyol. We were not the main club in the city. We can't say the same thing now.**"**

PABLO ZABALETA

a hero leaving the club sums up what has changed, May 2017

"Pablo teaches the new generation, the people who are coming in, what it means to be at the club, what it means to be in the Premier League, what many, many things mean.**"**

PEP GUARDIOLA

*sums up what Pablo Zabaleta meant to the
club when he left, May 2017*

"I am the Che Guevara of modern soccer."

SERGIO AGUERO

City's greatest ever goalscorer makes a bold claim, April 2017

" John has more personality than all of us in this room, more balls than everyone here. I like that player. **"**

PEP GUARDIOLA

has John Stones's back, September 2017

❝I played futsal and that helped me a lot. I used to play as a *goleiro-linha* – it's a goalkeeper who plays a lot with his feet… From that period, I had my shooting skills and good footwork.❞

EDERSON

gives the impression that he fancies playing up front, December 2017

" Countless of times have I imagined this day. After all, the end has felt nearby for so many years... Manchester City has given me everything. I've tried to give back as much as I possibly could... The time has come for me to go now. **"**

VINCENT KOMPANY

announces his City departure in May 2019

"Fernandinho is used to playing centre-midfield at centre-half. He can cruise the game. He's like a Rolls Royce... I was very impressed with him.**"**

MICAH RICHARDS

shows his faith in Fernandinho's versatility in September 2019

CHAPTER 4

VIEWS FROM THE TERRACES

"Blue Moon,
You saw me standing alone,
Without a dream in my heart,
Without a love of my own.**"**

CITY FANS'

anthem

"Niall Quinn's disco pants are the best,
They go up from his arse to his chest,
They're better than Adam and the Ants,
Niall Quinn's disco pants.**"**

CITY FANS'

*song, which originated after supporters spotted Quinn's fashionable
sartorial selection on a night out in the early 90s*

111

❝Are you watching,
Are you watching,
Are you watching,
Macclesfield?**❞**

CITY FANS

react to the Blues' relegation to Division Two
with typical humour, May 1998

"And all the runs that Kinky
makes are winding,
And all the goals that City score are blinding,
There are many times that we would
like to score again,
But we don't know how, because maybe,
You're gonna be the one that saves me,
And after all, you're my Alan Ball.**"**

SUPPORTERS'

version of Oasis' "Wonderwall", 1996

" We'll score again,
Don't know where,
Don't know when,
But I know we'll score again
Some sunny day. **"**

CITY FANS

lighten up a goal drought, October 1995

114

> **❝**Feed the Goat,
> Feed the Goat,
> Feed the Goat and he will score,
> Feed the Goat and he will score.**❞**

CITY FANS'

vocal tribute to Shaun Goater

" No matter what, skill will always prevail. There is no rule that says a footballer needs to be 'this high' and 'this wide'. I don't consider myself as a star. If you win without sacrifice you enjoy it, but it's more satisfying when you have struggled. **"**

PHIL FODEN

inspirational on and off the pitch, 2021

" City are the best team in the country with a manager considered to be the best in the world. It's a dream come true to be part of this club. **"**

JACK GREALISH

on becoming Britain's first £100m player, August 2021

❝You're just a fat Micah Richards,
Fat Micah Richards,
You're just a fat Micah Richards. **❞**

CITY FANS

welcome Arsenal's William Gallas in their own inimitable way, 2008

" 'Cos we've got [clap, clap]
Guardiola!
We've got [clap, clap]
Guardiola!
We've got [clap, clap]
Guardiola!
So glad you're mi-i-ne! **"**

CITY FANS

feeling "Glad all over" as City stroll to the Premier League title, April 2018

"Fergie, sign him up!"

CITY FANS

taunt United for letting Carlos Tevez go, 2010

❝We knew we could play the game of our lives tonight and still be on the end of a hammering.❞

NIGEL CLOUGH

the Burton Albion boss, who had just watched City beat his team 9–0 in the 2019 Carabao Cup semi-final first leg

CHAPTER 5

IN THE BOARDROOM

"The problem? I can't drag the old boots on anymore and get out on the park and play. It would be a lot easier if I could.**"**

FRANCIS LEE

surveys the work ahead as new chairman of City, February 1994

❝I see myself as a friendly advisor, not a dictator. ❞

FRANCIS LEE

answers accusations of interfering in team affairs, February 1994

"I will still be coming to matches –
mind you, I might have to wear a beard,
dark glasses and a dirty raincoat. **"**

FRANCIS LEE

shortly after standing down as chairman, March 1998

"Pep always has a knack for talent and he loves to find young players who have incredible talent. He finds that talent, he nurtures it and you find them evolve and really succeed.**"**

KHALDOON AL-MUBARAK
the City chairman welcomes Guardiola, June 2016

❝The finest-tuned athlete football has ever seen. So when we talk about Colin Bell, we talk about someone very special.**❞**

PETER SWALES

former chairman, 1979

"Pep wants to win it all and that's what I love about him most because that's how I feel too.**"**

KHALDOON AL-MUBARAK

City chairman and City coach – philosophies
in perfect alignment, June 2016

129

❝I remember him as one of the most likeable men I have ever known. He was a super character. In all the years I knew him, I never heard anyone say a bad thing about him – and that's unusual in our business.**❞**

FREDDIE PYE

ex-vice chairman, remembers Joe Mercer, 1990

“I am the boss at Maine Road and the manager knows it.**”**

PETER SWALES

former chairman

"I thought if we gave Malcolm Allison the right amount of money… he would be the most successful manager City had ever seen."

PETER SWALES

following Allison's sacking, 1980

"From time to time I find a City fan who tells me 'I've been through all the ups and downs. More downs than ups'. And the typical expression is: 'I was in Macclesfield'. If everybody who told me they were in Macclesfield really was in Macclesfield, they would have filled Wembley Stadium!**"**

FERRAN SORIANO

City's CEO looks back on tougher times, March 2016

"My biggest problem was that I should have interfered more. There were times when I should have been a bit stronger and said, 'Sorry, I don't agree with that,' and been stubborn about certain things. But I didn't. That's life.**"**

FRANCIS LEE

reflects on his time as chairman, 1998

❝Over the years Manchester City have had some fabulous players but Colin Bell is the best player I've seen in a Manchester City shirt. **❞**

PETER SWALES

1979

"Everyone will have their own experience of what happened. I don't think any league will be decided like that for many years to come. Maybe some people imagined it was 'typical City'. We are not 'typical City'. We have destroyed that thought. This is not a team that is going to lie down. Now we want to forget about 'typical City'.**"**

City Chairman **KHALDOON AL-MUBARAK** *comments on the extraordinary Premier League title win, May 2012*

"[City's] ambitions are large and unlimited.**"**

City owner **SHEIKH MANSOUR**
on City's future, November 2013

137

CHAPTER 6

IT'S GREAT TO BE A CITIZEN

> **"** I had a call from England coach Clive Woodward and I thought, it must be about selection, but he was just ringing to see if I was watching City on the box! **"**

WILL GREENWOOD

England rugby union star and City fan, February 2002

140

" The name I went with had nothing to do with thinking I was the best fighter on the Kippax or the biggest wit. Colin Bell was always known as 'The King of the Kippax', so that was the best name for the fanzine. **"**

DAVE WALLACE

editor of the City fanzine, August 2001

❝If I wasn't praying for City,
just think where we might be.**❞**

MCFC chaplain **TONY PORTER**

❝I felt at home from the first moment I arrived. That's why I signed for City.**❞**

EYAL BERKOVIC

July 2001

❝Which is my favourite? It has to be 'Feed the Goat'. City fans originated it so I'd go with that. **❞**

SHAUN GOATER

August 2001

"The game I remember best was the sixth round replay against Everton on the way to the 1981 FA Cup Final. Every time I got the ball those fans made me feel I could go past anyone.**"**

TOMMY HUTCHISON

on playing in front of the Kippax terrace, April 1994

The fans are absolutely unbelievable at this club and I owe them so much.

GIO KINKLADZE

1997

146

"I am very happy at this club
and my family are enjoying life here too.
When my mother came to visit, she did not
want to go back!**"**

ELANO AND FAMILY

preferring Mancunian drizzle to Rio, 2008

"In the Premier League, Champions League and any competitions, we end up facing all kinds of players. Our mindset is always the same: take one game at a time, treat every game like a Final. Only like that can our team succeed.**"**

RUBEN DIAS

April 2021

148

**❝What did I think of the
'Welcome to Manchester' poster? I liked it –
it made me laugh because it reminds me of
the rivalry we have in Argentina.
Funny and very healthy.❞**

CARLOS TEVEZ

lends his view of City's evocative poster campaign
shortly after his arrival from United, October 2009

149

❝I will never forget how I have been treated here by the fans, the club and the owners, and nothing would give me greater pleasure than to finish my career as a Manchester City player.❞

YAYA TOURE

at 31 years young Yaya signs for four more years, April 2013

"I thought if they call us the noisy neighbours then let's make more noise in the city, let's prove that we are a club that is looking to achieve important things, maybe one day be the main club in the city and take this club forward to the next step to make this club better.**"**

PABLO ZABALETA

looks back on his nine years at City, May 2017

"I miss the fans in England…
I don't miss the food, or the time or [the]
matter of driving, but the City fans, yes,
I miss them. **"**

MARIO BALOTELLI

reflects on his time at City, February 2014

❝I want City's supporters to know this:
When I heard them chant my name it
gave me a really warm feeling inside.
Sometimes I don't smile outwardly
but I am smiling inside.**❞**

MARIO BALOTELLI

explains his po-faced expressions

"There is a real soul about this club, a great work ethic, and if people want us to fail, so what? We are in the elite now.**"**

VINCENT KOMPANY

September 2010

154

❝The owners aren't just investing in the team, they are investing in the whole club, the training facilities, the stadium, the fans and the city of Manchester itself. They know how important City are to the people of Manchester and there is much more going on at the club than just creating a team.**❞**

VINCENT KOMPANY

September 2010

155

CHAPTER 7

GREAT
MOMENTS

"I am happy for the fans, they deserved to win this Cup. For a long time they didn't win. My feeling is good, but it's important that they feel good [too].**"**

ROBERTO MANCINI

delights in City's 2011 FA Cup win

❝It has been 44 years since this club last had their hands on the title and everyone at City knows that is too long. We did it the hard way but I am told that is the City way. The supporters have never lost faith or patience – even in the last five minutes today – and we are so pleased that this season, we have delivered some history for them.**❞**

ROBERTO MANCINI

after winning the Premier League title in astounding fashion, May 2012

159

❝We have beaten United two times, we have scored more than them and conceded less so we deserve it. I never gave up. It was a crazy finish to the game and the season but the best team won the title.**❞**

ROBERTO MANCINI

revels in pipping United to the Premier League title, May 2012

 **I just wellied it!** "

IAN BRIGHTWELL

explains the intricacies of his awesome strike at Old Trafford, February 1990

❝ It's the stuff dreams are made of and no matter what else I do in my career, I always have that. **❞**

PAUL DICKOV

recalls his last-gasp equaliser in the 1999 Play-Off Final,
February 2002

" When I was nine or ten, I had a chat
with my coach, and I asked if I could play in
goal. I started playing as a goalkeeper
and it was love at first sight.
Only a goalkeeper knows how it is. **"**

EDERSON

talking soon after joining City, as only a goalkeeper knows how,
August 2017

&&I knew as soon as I hit it, it was going in. I could tell by the sound. I caught it perfectly. The ball was in the back of the net almost before Peter Shilton took off.**&&**

NEIL YOUNG

remembers his 1969 FA Cup Final-winning goal, 2001

" Before the game, honestly, I thought I was going to score. I came close a few times. It's a bit of luck on the day, but also self-belief as well. **"**

VINCENT KOMPANY

City's skipper, the Carabao Cup final Man of the Match and goalscorer reflects on the afternoon, February 2018

❝When they hit the post for the fourth time, I thought it could just be our day.**❞**

JOE ROYLE

after City's dramatic promotion victory over Blackburn, May 2000

"Lesser mortals would have snatched at the chance, but he was the right person at the right moment for Manchester City and that's the only explanation I can give for what happened actually happening.**"**

MARTIN TYLER

the Sky Sports legend on his famous Aguerooooo moment,
May 2021

CHAPTER 8

GLORY DAYS

The past was yours, but the future's ours.

LIAM GALLAGHER

casting a beady eye across the city, February 2018

ffFancy a great strapping
fellow like me fainting in front of all
those people and the King. **JJ**

FRANK SWIFT

legendary goalkeeper, shortly after City lifted the FA Cup, April 1934

171

❝I've been in this game 47 f*****g years. I thought I'd seen every way in which a goal could be given away – but you just found another.**❞**

JOE MERCER

lets goalkeeper Harry Dowd into his thoughts after his error against WBA in a League Cup tie, October 1966

"We were one of the best sides of the last 50 years and, when we were flying, we were unstoppable.**"**

MIKE DOYLE

on the City team of the late 1960s

> **"** He has made us.
> He is something special.
> He is the best coach in the game. **"**

MIKE SUMMERBEE

on Malcolm Allison, February 1969

&&There were no team talks except for when Harry Dowd was playing, who wasn't the slightest bit interested in football – he'd rather have been doing plumbing or something. Joe [Mercer] would say, 'Harry, we're playing Arsenal today and they play in red and white.'**99**

MIKE SUMMERBEE

1990

❝I have to hold my hands up.
I cost Manchester City the
1972 League Championship.**❞**

RODNEY MARSH

after joining City during a run-in which saw them lose the title by one point

" Get him off, skip. He's gone. **"**

RODNEY MARSH

advises Tony Book to substitute Denis Law
after his goal relegated United, April 1974

177

"We do everything quick and simple and we're remarkably fit. We don't mind who comes to watch us train or play. We feel it's a simple game and we try and make it simple.**"**

JOE MERCER

1967

❝You lucky lot of b******s!
What a way to earn a living.**❞**

JOE MERCER

shares his thoughts with the City players, 1968

"I am a scientist.
My training is brilliant and, like all scientists,
I can make things work.**"**

MALCOLM ALLISON

January 1979

"You're not a good player.
In fact, you're a bad player.
But I could make you into a fair player.**"**

MALCOLM ALLISON

introduces himself to Frannie Lee, October 1967

"Four years ago it was all Man United, Man United, Man United. It drove me mad. If I mentioned Man City, they laughed at me. Who's laughing now?**"**

MALCOLM ALLISON

enjoying City's late-1960s dominance, June 1969

❝Before we won the Championship, I told the lads exactly how many goals we would score and how many points. I was exactly right. I'm brilliant!**❞**

MALCOLM ALLISON

modest as ever, November 1972

"It's an amazing feeling... Everyone has put his ego on the side."

SAMIR NASRI

sums up the team spirit that earned City the Premier League title, May 2014

"I think that big teams cannot be
be satisfied with just one title.
We have two titles in the year;
on Tuesday we start working
for next season.**"**

MANUEL PELLEGRINI

makes it clear there is no rest for the champions, May 2014

" Football could live without Joe Mercer, but Joe Mercer couldn't live without football. **"**

JOE MERCER

1972

" The league is won, now it's the records. The numbers keep the players focused. **"**

PEP GUARDIOLA

finding motivation for his players after winning the Premier League championship so early, April 2018

❝Today, there was a little bit of frustration because everyone was saying, 'Don't shoot! Don't shoot!' I could really hear it and it was annoying me.**❞**

VINCENT KOMPANY

after ingnoring his team-mates and smashing a 30-yarder to beat Leicester City in May 2019

188

"I grew up here and saw this stadium get built. It's a massive dream come true to win trophies here. It shows what the manager is building here. He said we needed to get the mentality right and we did that and did it exceptionally well.**"**

RAHEEM STERLING

after City completed a domestic treble with the 2019 FA Cup

"We are champions because we deserve to be. Because we are very, very fit, there is a lot of team spirit and we have allowed people to express themselves naturally. We work hard and we play positively. And the players we have – and we must not forget that these are the men who really did it – are better than even we realised.**"**

JOE MERCER

May 1968

190

ff It was an incredible final for us
and we have finished an incredible year.
To all the people at the club a big
congratulations, especially the players
because they are the reason why we have
won these titles. **JJ**

PEP GUARDIOLA

*celebrates the historic treble after the Blues' 6–0 rout of Watford
in the 2019 FA Cup final*

" This has been a season and a Premier League title like no other. This was the hardest one. We will always remember this season for the way that we won. I am so proud to be the manager here and of this group of players. **"**

PEP GUARDIOLA

celebrates City's third Premier League title in four years, May 2022